To:

_____

From:

_____

D1510309

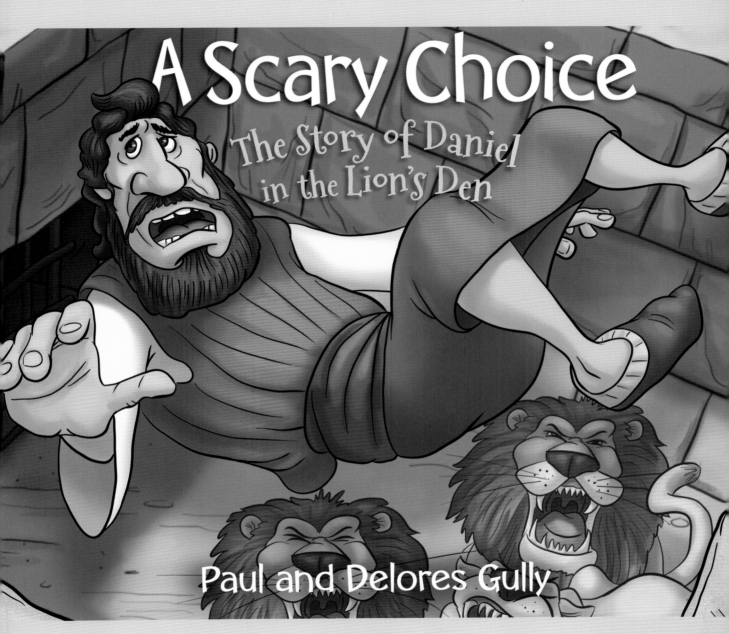

A Scary Choice

The Story of Daniel in the Lion's Den

Paul and Delores Gully

BroadStreet
KIDS

Published by BroadStreet Kids
BroadStreet Kids is an imprint of

BroadStreet Publishing® Group, LLC
Savage, Minnesota USA
BroadStreetPublishing.com

A Scary Story: The Story of Daniel in the Lion's Den

Written and illustrated by Paul & Delores Gully

ISBN 978-1-4245-5769-1 (hardcover)
ISBN 978-1-4245-5770-7 (ebook)

Stock or custom editions of BroadStreet Publishing titles may be purchased in bulk for educational, business, ministry, fundraising, or sales promotional use. For information, please e-mail info@broadstreetpublishing.com.

Printed in China

18 19 20 21   5 4 3 2 1

This true
story is from
Daniel 6 in
the Bible.

Daniel was a godly man,
a favorite of the king.
He had to make a scary choice.
Could you do such a thing?

His excellence and faithfulness
no one could deny.
Others envied his success,
and planned how he could die.

Daniel knelt and prayed to God,
morning, noon, and night.
He offered thanks and made requests
in everybody's sight.

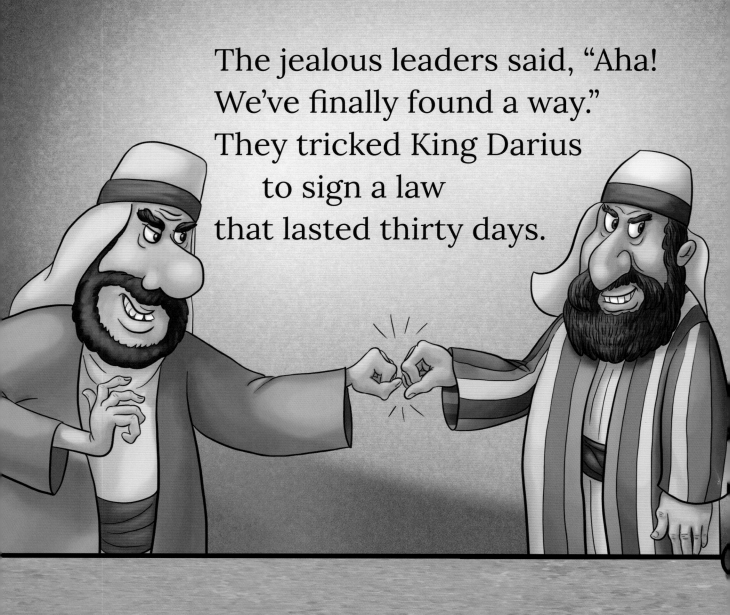

The jealous leaders said, "Aha!
We've finally found a way."
They tricked King Darius
to sign a law
that lasted thirty days.

When Daniel heard the dreadful news,
he had a choice to make.
"I only want to pray to God,
so this law I will break."

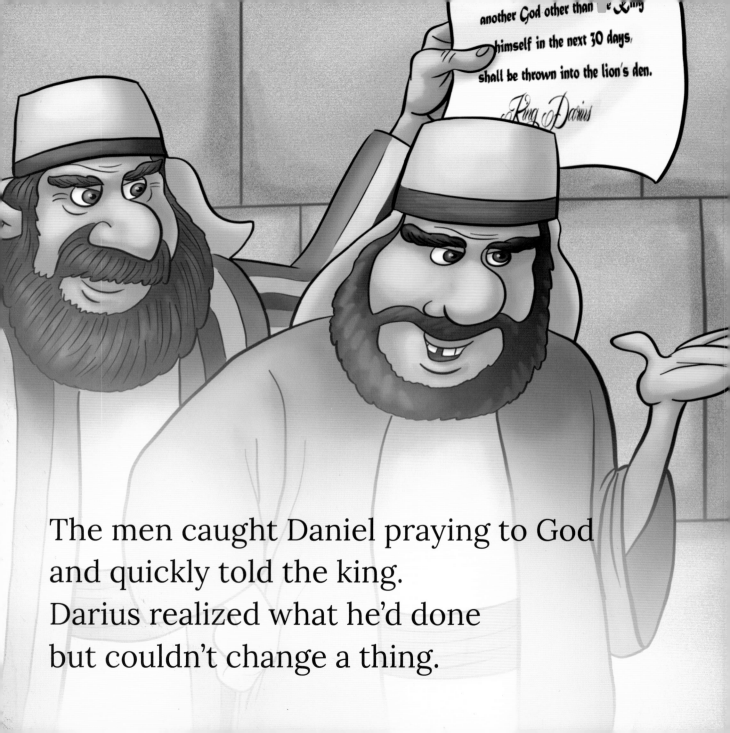

The men caught Daniel praying to God
and quickly told the king.
Darius realized what he'd done
but couldn't change a thing.

All day long he tried to find
a way to save his friend.
The leaders then reminded him,
"He must go in the den!"

King Darius shared his parting words:
"God be with you tonight."
And as they threw him in the den,
"Don't let the lions bite!"

The king went home and couldn't sleep.
He chose no food or fun.
His mind was filled with scary thoughts.
Was Daniel's life now done?

Daniel waited in the dark
as the lions roared.
An angel came and shut their mouths—
a meal he was no more.

King Darius ran to the den
as the sun arose.
He found that God had saved his friend.
He still had all his toes!

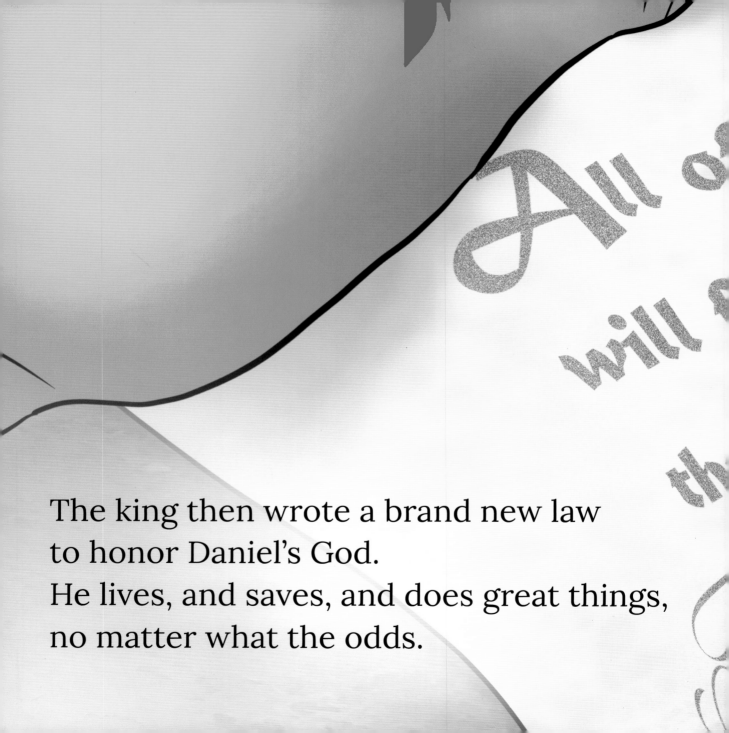

The king then wrote a brand new law
to honor Daniel's God.
He lives, and saves, and does great things,
no matter what the odds.

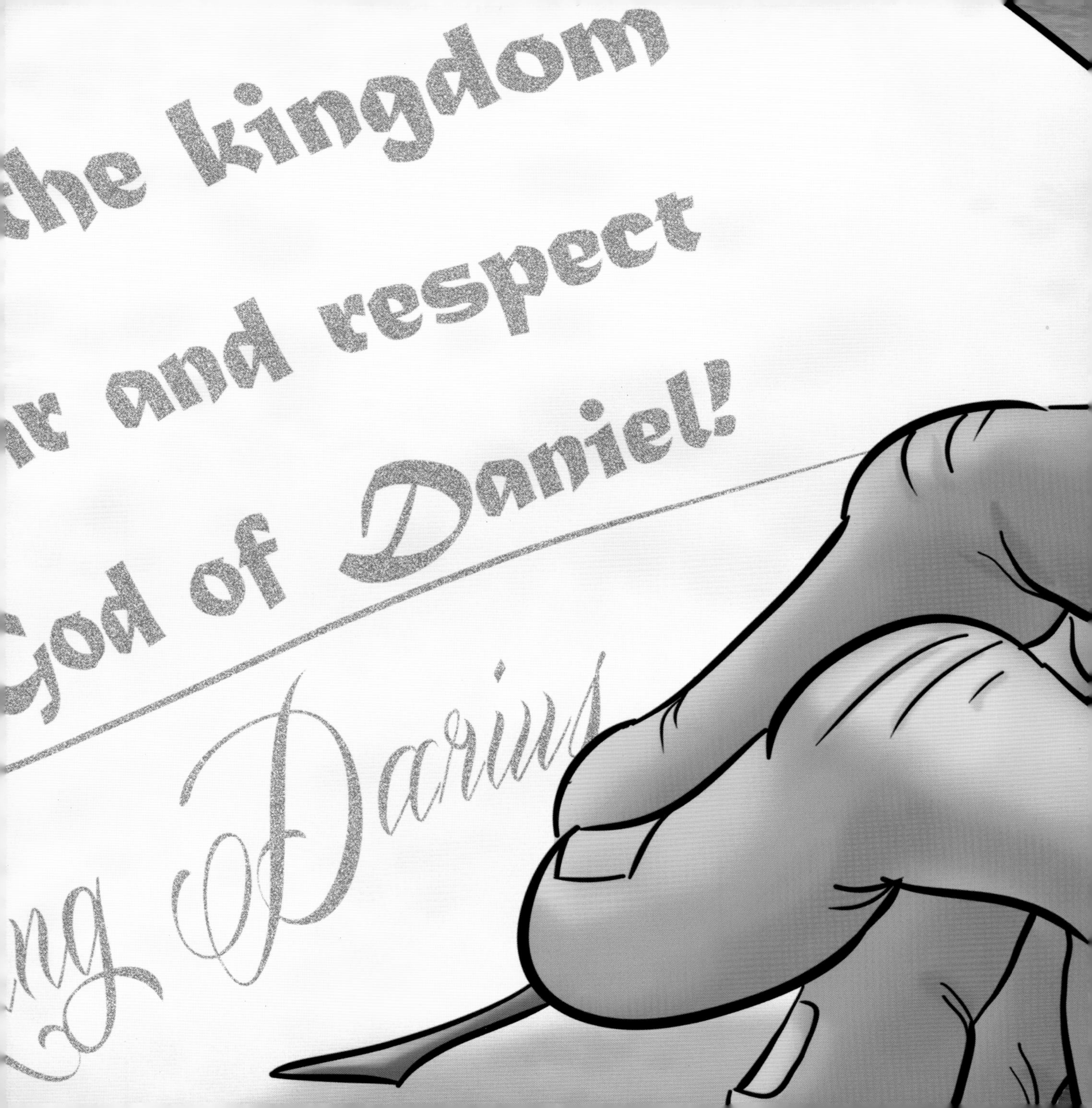
the kingdom
r and respect
God of Daniel!
ng Darius

Daniel made a scary choice;
you'll have choices too.
Trust in God with all your heart.
He'll be there for you.

Paul and Delores Gully currently reside near the Twin Lakes of DeFuniak Springs in Florida. They met while attending Ringling College of Art and Design where Delores mistook Paul for one of his identical triplet brothers, who was in her class. Their God-given talent has been utilized to illustrate books and curriculum worldwide. Their passion is to help children understand how much God loves them. They enjoy traveling, hiking, fishing, reading, bicycling, and watching action movies.

Connect with the Gullys at PaulGullyIllustrator.com and Facebook.com/pvggraphicsanddesign.

Enjoy another great Bible story!